Coaching Youth Baseball:
COACH LIKE A CHAMPION

DREW COOLIDGE

DEDICATED TO MY FAMILY

This book has been in the works since I was first born and is dedicated to my family. Mom, Dad, Bette, Margie, Christopher, Steve, Sandi, Abbie and Grace...can't thank you all enough for who you are.

TABLE OF CONTENTS

Introduction   i

COACH
LIKE A
CHAMPION

INTRODUCTION

I would like to thank all of my coaches, teammates and players from throughout the years. Baseball is truly an amazing game that reaches people throughout the world. My experiences with all of you have shaped me into who I am today.

Jeff and Dan, two teammates who are now with God much too early, thank you for all the memories and may you enjoy the best seat in His house.

There is something truly special about baseball. The sound of the ball hitting the bat. The sound of the pitch crashing into the catcher's glove. The sound of sunflower seeds being eaten or stepped on. The sound of the crowd. The sound of the umpire. The sound of little brothers and sisters playing tag next to the bleachers. There's the smell of popcorn, of hot dogs, of wet grass during a rain delay. There's the joy of a hit, of a great play, of a victory and there's the hurt from making an error, from striking out, from not winning. No matter what, there is something truly special about baseball that reaches all of our senses.

To be a successful baseball coach, at any level, you must develop confidence in all of your players. When players believe in themselves amazing - truly amazing - things can happen. If players believe in themselves and if **all** players believe in **all** of their teammates,

miracles can happen. You are coaching America's Pastime and are responsible for America's Future. Thank you for buying this book! Not only will you learn great situational drills for players of all ages, you will also learn how to be a strategic coach in games.

I know there are many good books out there about drills and practices. And, if actual games were all about how to perform those drills...you would certainly have the best "practice team." What makes this book different from the rest is you will learn how to incorporate game situations into the drills during practice PLUS you will learn how to manage your team during games. Have a baseball notebook ready and you will be on your way to the most successful season you have ever coached!

Coaching Youth Baseball

COACH LIKE A CHAMPION

Coaching America's Pastime...
Responsible for America's Future

Drew Coolidge

WHY COACH?

"If you don't know where you are going, you might wind up someplace else." - Yogi Berra

Coaching is one of the most rewarding experiences you will ever have if you are in it for the right reasons. If you want to help someone succeed, help someone become his very best and help create memories for many...then, you are in it for the right reasons! Coaching baseball can also be the most fun you have ever had. Calling the right pitch for the final out, calling for the perfect bunt at the perfect time and placing your players in the right spot to succeed will keep you smiling through the night. There really are few things better than watching your team celebrate in victory or watching your team carry themselves like champions in defeat.

When you are finished reading this book your brain will have new ideas to take with you to the diamond. You will have a better idea how to define success, simplify the game and you will be the coach who all the players will want to play for and all parents will want their child to learn from. Now, that you are ready to become your very best, let's look at what you can do to get the best out of your players!

FOR THE BULLPEN IN YOUR BRAIN: John Wooden is one of the greatest coaches of all time - in any sport - and he offered this to all the coaches in the world, *"Make sure that team members know they are working with you, not for you."*

WARM-UP:
WHAT IS YOUR PLAN?

At all ages, baseball is a human chess match. As the coach, you need to **always** have a plan for each practice and each game. Each plan needs to have a goal to be reached. You have probably heard that baseball is a game of failure and your coaching style, all of the time, needs to reflect how to succeed even when you fail. If you are going to yell at a player after he strikes out or after he makes an error in the field, then you may reconsider coaching. When a player makes an error or doesn't get a hit he already doesn't feel the greatest about himself. So, have it in your plan to inspire players all of the time...good and bad.

Back to baseball being a game of failure...and, failure in this case is not being negative at all. It's just the way baseball is! If a hitter's batting average (BA) is .300 that means he fails seven out of 10 times. However, he is still an amazing hitter! So, how are you prepared to help that player when he doesn't get a hit those seven times? If you haven't already planned how to deal with failure, then now is the perfect time to start. The earlier you can get the team to work with you and buy into the fact that it is okay to fail...the sooner you will start preparing them to be their very best. Not just in baseball but in life.

President George W. Bush's "No Child Left Behind Act" established in 2001 emphasized teaching methods that were proven to work for students. The Individualized Education Plan (IEP) came to be so disadvantaged students were given tools to succeed. Without probably realizing it, the very best coaches use the IEP concept and you should, too. You can teach a concept to the entire team and each player will understand it a little differently than the player standing next to him. You need to really pay attention to how each player on your team learns and focus on that in <u>every</u> practice and in <u>every</u> game. If you can do that you will maximize each player's potential. I call it the Individualized Baseball Plan (IBP). When you are able to plan each practice and each game around <u>all</u> of your players' IBPs, you will succeed and each of your players will succeed. What a great feeling!

FOR THE BULLPEN IN YOUR BRAIN: Are you determined to **always** plan so you can be your very best and so your players can be their very best? Hall of Famer Tommy Lasorda said, *"The difference between the impossible and the possible lies in a man's determination."*

PREGAME:
WHAT ARE YOUR GOALS?

Your warm-up establishes the plan and now you must set your goals. This is huge! When you are coaching baseball, a game that is based on failure, you must set goals that can be reached **all** of the time. If you work hard enough, you and your players will achieve the goals. And, based on each player's IBP, you must set a goal specifically for each. You will be blessed with a stud shortstop, pitcher or catcher and his goals will be different than the player who is in his first year of baseball.

For players ages 5-10 the goals should be different from those who are 11-14. And, those 11-14 should have different goals from those who are 15-19 years old. Set a few **simple** goals for the season's first practice to establish the accomplishment of achieving goals. Having fun, catching with two hands, stepping to your target, throwing with four seams...these are all goals that can be reached. It is important for you to tell the team their goals before practice and summarize how you reached them at the end of practice.

Now, these may seem like simple goals but when you and your team accomplish these in the first practice then you are on your way! The first practice sets the stage for the rest of the season and it can either go well or the players and parents may be calling for relief from the 'pen before you know it. Because baseball is a game of failure it needs time to balance itself. Set your goals accordingly knowing that you want each player to get better at every practice and in every game, building on the past foundations you've set and reaching for the peak at the end of the season.

FOR THE BULLPEN IN YOUR BRAIN: *"Things turn out best for the people who make the best of the way things turn out."* - John Wooden

PREGAME CONTINUED:
WHAT IS SUCCESS?

We've had our warm-up, started our pregame and before we jump to the game, we need to define success. We will get into the game and its situations in just a little bit. If you are not patient and just want to play games then baseball may not be for you! That is probably the #1 problem with coaches and players today is that they just want to get out and play without a plan and without a clear definition of success. These are the coaches who may - or may not - realize they are discouraging players from America's Pastime...and future. They don't make time to plan, set goals and define success. It is more true in baseball than in any other sport (except maybe golf) that winning is not everything. As a coach, you must always develop your players and you need to develop as a coach as well.

In case you missed it, baseball is a game of failure and it needs time to balance itself. For example, if a player grounds out seven times in a row to start the season he is hitting .000. Then, if he gets a hit in his next three at-bats he is suddenly hitting .300! Baseball is tough and you need to teach patience. It is a game so similar to life that you must prepare your entire team to be successful on and off the field. Baseball needs time to balance itself...and, as a coach, you need to trust the game and its quirks.

If your goal is to win every single baseball game...what happens when you run into a pitcher who flat-out owns the zone and shuts you down? That's what happens in baseball. In football or basketball, you can call a game-winning play for your star player to execute. In baseball, you can't switch the lineup in the last inning so your best hitter comes up. You're dealt with whose turn it is and you make the most of it. Hopefully, you have planned and practiced for nearly every possible situation so the odds are in your favor. However, sometimes you win and sometimes you don't. That is why you have to define success.

Unless you are a college or professional coach, winning is not everything. This is another reason why you need to define success. You are blessed with the opportunity to coach - and, mentor - the future. If your **only** goal is to win then you have already failed. A few of the coaches you will face are more worried about how they appear to everyone when they lose than how their players can learn from defeat. This is where you can make an impressionable difference to your team and find success in everything you do. Set a goal to be the positive coach who never yells at the players or umpires. That style is contagious and your players and fans will act the same. Your team will be known for sportsmanship and that is simply awesome.

Success in baseball - at all ages - can always be found if you look for it other than on the scoreboard or in the scorebook. Imagine if success were defined as, *"Being better now than I was earlier - as a player and a person - and all my efforts are solely for the team."* As a coach, you need to believe and adhere to this just as you expect of your players.

Every baseball team has an ace. Every baseball team has its slugger. But, look at the championship baseball teams in the MLB, Japan, college or in your area. They have what the other teams don't have and that is a true leader as a coach, a team concept (that everyone believes in) and a specific plan. This is what you can establish at any age and it is what will make your players better people. Very few make it big in baseball so you need to establish each of your player's IBPs and help them make it big in life. Now, you have established a goal and a plan to be successful. The wins will take care of themselves.

FOR THE BULLPEN IN YOUR BRAIN: Establish an IBP for each of your players, and for yourself, based on your definition of success and pay attention to what works. As Yogi Berra once said, *"You can observe a lot by just watching."*

PRACTICE PART I:
PLANNING WITH A PURPOSE

Now that we have defined success we can apply it to everything from planning practice to playing games. In **simplest form**, there is no difference in Little League than in Major League. There are nine players on the field, one ball and both teams get three outs when they are hitting. The pitcher throws the ball, the batter tries to hit it and the defense tries to get an out.

When you plan practice, **keep it simple!** One problem some Little League, Pony League, High School and Legion coaches have is that they try to complicate everything. If you want to be the best coach you can be - for any age group - then I offer you this challenge: Record one MLB game on television, grab a scorebook, a notebook, a bottle of water, some sunflower seeds, **turn your cell phone off** and watch the entire game while keeping score and taking notes. It really is fun! Then, do the following:

- Write down how many times the pitcher threw the first pitch for a strike. At the end of the game, calculate the on-base-percentage for all those hitters who were down 0 balls and 1 strike. For example, the starting pitcher went 7.0 innings and faced 24 batters and threw a first-pitch strike to 19 of them. That is a great ratio and I would guess in those 19 at-bats only two - maybe three - managed to get a hit or get on base after being down in the count 0-1. The other starting pitcher went 6.1 innings and faced 29 batters and threw 13 first pitch strikes. The 16 first-ball batters he faced had a much better average because they started the count 1-0. Lessoned learned? Pitchers who can throw the first pitch for a strike have better odds at succeeding. Batters who can get a first-pitch ball have a better chance of getting on base. See?! It is pretty **simple!**

- Mark in the scorebook where a player hits a ball. See if that trend continues in each of his at-bats. If he hits to the left side, would you adjust your defense to play to those odds? I know I would based on the game situation. If he were the first guy up in an inning and his first two at-bats he hit up the middle I would have my shortstop and second baseman pinch a little bit closer to second base.

- Act like a scout while you are watching the game and make notes if a player tends to swing at the first pitch. If that's the case, notice how he's pitched in his next at-bat. The pitcher would probably throw it out of the zone, get him to swing and miss and quickly be up in the count 0-1. This is something you can do against the teams you play and you will be one step ahead of them all of the time. That is good planning.

- Make notes when stolen bases happen. What was the count? What was the situation? What batter was up and who was on deck? Maybe the batter was a slow runner and they wanted to avoid a double play. Maybe the guy on deck was seeing the ball well and had a good chance to knock in a runner from second base. When you break down a game you will be amazed at why professional and college coaches do what they do. It is **always** with a purpose. When I coach, if my runners can see that the pitcher is going to throw an off-speed pitch, they have a green light to steal in most situations. I prefer being aggressive and the odds are in our favor...even against great catchers.

- Make notes when a team bunts. Was it for a hit or a sacrifice? What was the count? Who was on deck? How fast was the runner on base? Was it done to change a pitcher's rhythm?

Here is my next challenge to you. Record a college game and do the exact same things! Baseball is one of the hardest sports to play but keep it in its **simplest form** and it is the most fun to coach. You can learn an awful lot by breaking down games on television and learning from them.

Now that you have done that, here is how you can apply what you have learned from MLB and college to your practices. Make note of all the situations in those games and incorporate those in everything you do. Your job is to prepare your players for success. Remember, success is *"Being better now than I was earlier - as a player and a person - and all my efforts are solely for the team."* Just by making time to study college and pro games you are already better and you did it for your team!

The standard defensive plays are groundouts, flyouts and strikeouts. So, hit situational ground balls to your infielders or hit fly balls to your outfielders with a purpose. For example, no outs and nobody on base. If you can get the first out of an inning then the odds are in your favor to keep your opponent scoreless that inning. What a great goal to set! Nearly 90% of runners reaching base before an out is made score that inning. So, **getting that first out is key**. Put a runner on second base with two outs and hit a ground ball in the hole and let your defense know that runner on second base simply cannot score no matter what. This situation shows the infielders that they must do everything possible to keep the ball from getting through to the outfield.

Incorporating game situations into your practice is fun, keeps everyone active and prepares your players for the next game. Take it to a new level each time by adding detailed situations with a purpose. For example, a situation that comes up a lot of times at the younger ages is that the defense tends to panic when runners are on base and they almost always try to get the lead runner out. Well, if you are up by five runs then just try to get the easiest out even if it means sacrificing a run. These are situations that need to be practiced, too. If you don't, the players may always try to get the lead runner and before you know it the game will be tied. Always have situational practices as if you had the lead **and** as if you were behind. The results will start to show on the field. The more the players have practiced a situation the more they will know what to do when it happens in a game. And, this only takes a few minutes, each and every practice, so be sure to plan for it.

There are sample practice plans coming up in a few pages for all ages. Each one incorporates the fundamentals that need to be practiced every day and situations to prepare for the games. There is a study that for athletes, who are 12-18 years old, to be their very best (and, remember each player is different in his abilities) they need to do that activity 10,000 times. That means, 10,000 ground balls straight on. 10,000 ground balls to their right. 10,000 to their left. 10,000 on the run. Hitting 10,000 inside fastballs, 10,000 outside fastballs and 10,000 curveballs, etc. This work should be done mostly in the off-season so the regular season can be to fine-tune all the fundamentals and situations.

If you are coaching 5-19 year olds you do not have the same amount of time to prepare as college or professional teams. Your practices probably run one, maybe two hours. Most coaches will take an infield, an outfield, batting practice and have a bullpen session or two. That is always good but no where in that schedule are you working on situations that your players will see in a game.

Whatever time you have for practice, make sure at least 19% of it is dedicated to situations. You will see far greater rewards.

FOR THE BULLPEN IN YOUR BRAIN:

"It's the little details that are vital. Little things make big things happen." - John Wooden

PRACTICE PART II:
GET ON BASE AND SCORE!

When you are planning for offense you must **keep it simple**, too.
When you watched the recorded MLB and college games you may
have noticed not one single batter hit the same way as another. Try
to remember that when you are teaching how to hit. **Keep it simple,**
fun and with a purpose. Each player will be comfortable with a
certain swing and your job is to make sure they are focused on one
thing... putting the ball in play. You can work on their grip (making
sure their middle knuckles on both hands are lined up correctly so
their wrists are free to explode to the ball), work on their weight
(staying back as long as they can before exploding to the ball) and
work on their eyes (so their head is free to see the ball coming in),

but what really matters, in simplest form, is **putting the ball in play**.

In a 7-inning game each team gets 21 outs. Wouldn't it be nice to have more outs than the team you are playing?! Well, here is another way to look at this to increase how many outs you get. Those 21 outs are based on either a fly ball or a strikeout. If the batter hits a fly ball the defender has one chance to catch it and it is an out. So, if the team hits 21 fly balls then the defense has 21 chances to make the out. However, if the batter hits a ground ball there are three more chances you have to get on base; the fielder has to field it cleanly, throw it accurately and then it has to be caught before the runner gets to the base. Just by hitting a ground ball you now have increased your outs to 63 outs if every batter hit it on the ground. Lesson learned? Avoid strikeouts and fly outs and force the other team to make the play.

Make a point to plan time for running the bases in your practice. If you were able to videotape one of your games and break it down pitch-by-pitch and play-by-play you will notice areas where you can improve your team's baserunning. Keep in mind that today's youth are incredible visual learners. So, show them how to run the bases correctly. Then, have the players do it at 75% speed so you can confirm they are doing it correctly before they run it at 101%. Finally, incorporate what they learned in a situation that would happen in a game. Most coaches will just run a few drills, which is important, but you can take it to a new level by **simply** incorporating situations so they are fully prepared in the games to succeed. Create some games, relays and timed running events...kids love all of these!

Teach your players to sprint all the way through first base with no hesitations. As soon as they touch the base have them look to their right to see if the ball got away from the first baseman. I have taught this at the earliest of ages and they can do it as well as teenagers. It is a great way to turn an infield ground ball into a double (or, statistically a two-base error). Teach your runners to run from first to second and to stay on the base. Then, run from first to third and look for the third base coach 10-15 feet before second base for the sign to keep on running or the sign to stay at second base. Finally, work on scoring from second base with no hesitation at third. This is a great situational drill to get that extra run with two outs in an inning.

As you are planning your situational practices always remember to practice as if it were a game. Have you ever noticed - especially in Little League but really at all youth levels - baseball players aren't always comfortable in their uniforms at the beginning of the season? It is because they are not used to wearing them. So, to simplify the game-day jitters, have your players practice in baseball pants, cleats and hats. Start that discipline the first practice and it won't be an issue. If you try to incorporate it later in the season it is too late. You can't *always* teach young kids new tricks!

Start your practices with the same warm-up routine as you would before a game. Have pitchers throw with catchers, shortstops throw with second basemen, third baseman throw with the first baseman and outfielders throw with outfielders. **Keep it as simple** and as seamless as possible to keep those pregame jitters to a minimum. The reason athletes choke is they are not prepared. It is that **simple**. If you have your athletes prepared then you have already succeeded and a scoreboard victory is just icing on the cake. I can't tell you how many times I have watched athletes of all ages and all sports and unfortunately witnessed someone choke in a pressure situation. Usually, in the post-game interview the quote will be, "That was the first time I have been in that situation. I will learn from it." Well, perhaps the coach did not do his job in preparing his team other than understanding it was a learning situation. If that player had been in a similar, simulated situation the odds would have been in his favor. Whatever happens will happen but those who are prepared are those who will succeed the most.

Finish your practices with how to properly shake hands, thank the umpires and develop even more good sportsmanship habits. A game should not be the first time your team works on its sportsmanship. Your team should win and lose as champions and that responsibility falls entirely on the coach.

FOR THE BULLPEN IN YOUR BRAIN: "I talked to the players and tried to make them aware of what was good and bad, but I didn't try to run their lives." - John Wooden

PLAYING PART I:
BECOMING A STRATEGIC COACH

Obviously, this is the best part of any sport...especially baseball! When it is time to finally play ball, keep your approach **simple** and see how preparing for every situation slows down the pace of the game and will make you and your team successful. As a coach, this is where you can make a difference in this human chess match. As a coach, this is also where you can lose a game by trying to do too much.

Make a point **before** every game you coach, make a point **during** every game you coach and make a point **after** every game you coach to remember when you once played and how much fun it was supposed to be. **For 99% of the players, winning is not**

everything. Give a losing player a few minutes after the loss and he will move on to what's next on his daily agenda. Coaches and parents tend to take losses much harder. Make it fun for everyone. This is a discipline.

If you have fully prepared your entire team, based on their IBPs, based on how to react in situations during the game then most likely you will be in a position to win most games. You do not need the most talented team to win. You need the most prepared team to win. And, that is all on your shoulders, Coach!

My high school coach, Rick Harig, led our team to consecutive appearances in the American Legion World Series. Not many players in the history of Legion ball can say that they played back-to-back years in the ultimate of all tournaments. Coach Harig led us there by keeping our approach **simple**, staying positive and using key words to keep our focus and to remind us what to do in certain situations. As a middle infielder, coach would say one word to me when there was a runner on second base with two outs. This word reminded me to do whatever it took to keep the ball from getting to the outfield so that runner could not score. **Come up with trigger words when you are practicing situations and say them when situations arise in games.** Your players will say, "Oh yea. Now I remember what to do."

In college at Chapman University, Mike Weathers (who is now retired from being the Head Coach at Long Beach State) had shirts made for us with "Ag-Ack" on the back. We all said "Ag-Ack" and it brought us together. It was our thing. Now, in my 23rd year of coaching, I still say "Ag-Ack." When I say it, the team knows it is time to focus. Plus, it is fun to have fans ask about what the heck we are saying! Most of the time I hear the players saying it to each other and that is a great feeling. They're learning to coach themselves. **A baseball game usually lasts two to three hours. However, the actual playing time is less than 19 minutes**. So, there is a lot of down time which can lead to losing focus. Ag-Ack and right back on track.

During games, there is a fine line between coaching and letting the players play the game. Coaches who are constantly coaching during a game rarely have successful teams. That type of coaching is for practices. Game coaching is totally different....it's strategic. If a player is getting yelled at or being coached during a game...how are they able to play relaxed so their true talents can shine? Think about this for a minute...how many times has a batter completely missed the first pitch and the coach immediately starts coaching him with what to do for the next pitch? If you are the batter you suddenly start thinking about where your hands need to be, where your weight needs to be and you are afraid to make an out...all because the coach was trying to do too much. With all those thoughts, how are you going to be your very best so you can have an opportunity to **put the ball in play** and hopefully get on base? Try saying the following if the batter misses the first pitch, "Way to be aggressive. You still have two more strikes, two more chances to crush the ball!" As a batter, this would fire me up to hear! Much better than telling me what to do which - as I should've been taught in practice - I already know why I just failed on the first pitch and don't want to think about my failures.

Pay attention to the coaches who always coach during games and you will see players thinking too much and not in a position to succeed. Baseball is hard enough as it is. **Putting too much in a player's head makes it nearly impossible. The players need to know you trust in their abilities so they can free their mind and let their body take over and just play ball.** Why do you think good coaches always say, "Just like in practice..." when a player goes up to the plate or out in the field?! It's to remind players they have done this before and it is the same thing. Now, imagine if you have practiced an exact situation and you can remind them of that so they can shine!

Keep a small notebook with you during games and make notes on what worked and what you need to work on during the next practice. The notebook is an incredible tool! If the opponent had a runner on second base and their batter drilled a ball to the gap and your centerfielder grabbed the ball at the fence and tried to throw the runner out at home...then, a good hitter/runner would take second base on the long throw. Why not prepare your outfielders to either hit their cutoff man or get the ball to second base and sacrifice that run? If an outfielder has to turn and run to the ball the chances of throwing out that runner trying to score at home are brutally minimal. Teach your team it is okay to give up a run - in certain situations - to prevent more runs from scoring. This way, you may give up one run but you keep the player who hit the ball at first base.

Now, you have a force at first base and second base and the odds are back in your favor. Avoid the big innings by playing smart. And, playing smart comes from perfectly practicing situations during practices.

One more observation for you...if the above situation happened during a game, most coaches would immediately yell at their centerfielder for making a silly throw. What good does this do? The centerfielder (and, the rest of the team) already feels down for giving up a run...don't make it worse. **In your notebook**, make a note of that situation so you can work on it at your next practice and give a quick reminder that if you have to turn your back to home plate then you probably won't be able to throw that runner out at home. So, throw it to second base as quickly and accurately as you can. Your job during the game is to have a great strategy **and** to keep your players in the right frame of mind to succeed.

PLAYING PART II:
GIVE ALL PLAYERS A CHANCE

In every level younger than high school or American Legion, do your best to make sure everyone has equal playing time over the course of the season. This is more difficult than it may sound but its reward is priceless and its consequences could be career-ending. In the history of baseball, **every single player** reaches that day when his baseball career is over. It is a fact that just happens. It may not happen until someone is in his late 30s or it may - unfortunately - happen before high school. However, it should **never** happen before the age of 15 because of a coach.

As a coach, buy a spiral notebook and designate a few pages in it for each of your players. Keep track of who starts each game and do your best to spread that honor. I wish there were a better label than, "The starting lineup." It leaves an impression that those who aren't in the lineup are not good enough. Even in high school, I call it, "The first nine to play *this* game." Then, I make an effort to remind those who aren't playing that they actually have an advantage - if they pay attention in the dugout - because they will have a chance to know what the other team's tendencies are when they get their chance to shine. Having this notebook also is documented proof to show a parent who may be complaining about playing time.

FOR THE BULLPEN IN YOUR BRAIN: During games become a "Strategic Coach" and a "Psychological Coach." A "Coaching Coach" is for practices.

COACHING THE PARENTS:
HARDEST PART OF COACHING

Probably the number one reason a coach does not stick around very long is because of having to deal with parents. Not all parents are hard to deal with but it only takes one to ruin a good coach. What is sad about this is usually the player does not feel the same as the parent and it is the player who gets hurt the most.

You need to establish the ground rules for the parents before the season starts or as early as possible. Do this in writing and even think about drawing up a contract for you and the parents. Do your best to let the parents know that during games they should not be in the dugout or be coaching from the bleachers. It is your job to coach. You don't go into their home and parent their child. They need to understand the same is true on the diamond. It is a lot easier said than done.

Ask all of the parents to cheer for every player on your team...not just for their own child. In all my years, I can't tell you how many players are hurt by the way their parents act in the bleachers. Imagine if you were playing shortstop (with a great view of the bleachers) and you saw most of the parents sitting together and then your parent(s) were off to the side on their own. As a player, you are expected to be part of the team and the same should be said of the parents.

When we won the 1987 and 1988 American Legion State Tournaments, then the American Legion Western Regional Tournaments and berths in the American Legion World Series our parents worked together as well as we did. It was amazing and we drew strength from them. In fact, in the 1988 Regional Championship game we were down by two runs with two outs in the 9th inning and nobody on base. There were players nearly in tears in our dugout because our dream of back-to-back World Series berths was one out away from being over. Parents from the other team were forming a line by the pay phone (there weren't many cell phones, yet) to reserve flights to the World Series. Our parents, however, did not feel that way. They were cheering and pumping us up. Guess what happened? We hit back-to-back homeruns to tie the game and won it in extra innings. Baseball needs time to balance itself. In this case, it needed extra innings.

In your meeting before the season with the parents, ask them to call, text or e-mail you to schedule a meeting if they have issues with the way you coach their child. Ask them never to yell at you in front of their child or in front of the team. Be sure they know they are only to ask questions about their own child and that every other player on the team is off-limits to them.

I have seen parents who think the world evolves around their child. This may possibly be okay at home (that is out of your control) but it does not fit well with a team. If that is what they want then recommend they have their child play golf or tennis. Baseball is a team sport like none other. You can't substitute in baseball like you can in football or basketball. Baseball's rules don't allow for that. As was mentioned earlier, in football or basketball you can call specific plays for the star player at any time. In baseball, you never know where the ball will be hit so you can't put your star player at every defensive position. And, you can't put your best hitter at-bat whenever you feel like it. Baseball is designed to be a team sport. There is not another sport like it.

A basketball coach I know tells his players they are not to talk about what happened at practice or in a game when they are home. This may seem harsh but it is also brilliant. By following this, it eliminates the chance a parent has to criticize or doubt a coach which can lead to the player doing the same. If a child sees a parent doing it then he thinks it is okay for him to do it. Again, I go back to the statement that a coach does not go into a home and tell a parent how to parent. A parent should never tell a coach how to coach. Unfortunately, a few parents do not see that side of it in today's society.

The more you can communicate with the parents the less you probably will have to deal with them. Keep them informed via e-mail, texts or phone calls about the plans for the week. Share with them what goals the team reached and what new goals are on the horizon. Ask them to help you reach those goals.

FOR THE BULLPEN IN YOUR BRAIN: As a coach, it is really tough to please everyone on your team...and, their parents. However, simply **preparing for every situation** and living by your definition of success will allow you to sleep at night instead of tossing and turning and wondering, "What if?" Today's society is not as accountable as it used to be and the blame is tossed before looking in the mirror. Unfortunately, those who blame others tend to flock together. So, do your best to take that option away from them and rise above it all. You can make a difference and be a positive influence - on players AND parents - while the negative few soak in their tears until they get tired of it.

"Little League baseball is a very good thing because it keeps the parents off the streets." - Yogi Berra

PRACTICE SCHEDULE:
PLAYERS 5-10 YEARS OLD

There are some baseball etiquettes and superstitions to talk about for all ages before the team steps on the field. The earlier these can be taught the more the Baseball Gods will shine on you and your team! First of all, never - absolutely never - step on the chalk when you're running on or off the field...in practice and in games. Watch the professionals, they will sometimes jump over the chalk lines! This is the chalk down each infield line and both outfield lines. Bad luck attacks if you touch the chalk and it is not worth the risk. Next, at the beginning of practice or before a game, never warm up on the infield. Always run and throw in the outfield closest to your dugout. Finally, when a baseball player steps on the field it is his time to forget about everything going on in his personal life and just focus on **simply** having fun and **simply** playing a game.

1-HOUR PRACTICE SCHEDULE

1- If you are using the third base dugout, jog to the left field corner then stay along the outfield fence and jog to the right field corner. Do this two or three times to get the blood flowing. Stretching cold muscles increases a chance of injury so get a little sweat going first. (3-5 minutes)

2- Get the team along the left field line, in a circle (or have three players lead the team and have lines of players facing them), and then go through a series of leg stretches, back stretches and arm stretches (arm circles going forward then backward starting small and getting bigger are great for this). Finish with 21 crunches (Roberto Clemente wore #21 and it can't hurt you to honor him!). (5 minutes)

3- Partner up, get on a knee (right handers on their right knee with the left one at a right angle and the kneecap pointing toward their partner and left handers on their left knee with the right knee at a right angle and the kneecap point toward their target) and lightly throw to start getting loose. After one minute of this stand up and increase the throwing distance. As well as getting loose, be sure the players are throwing using a 4 seam grip. This means the "horseshoe" of the baseball should be perpendicular to the players' fingers. Throwing with all 4 seams will keep the ball moving straight. The earlier a player can learn to grip the ball this way will help him tremendously throughout his playing days. Holding a ball with 2 seams (the "horseshoe" of the ball will be above his fingertips) will cause the ball to move more and not go as fast. Continue increasing the distance to make their arms stronger. (8-10 minutes)

4- Most of the teams in this age bracket have 12 players so now get into three groups of four players. Adjust accordingly based on how many players but try to keep even numbers so everyone has a partner. Station #1 will work on ground balls. Station #2 will work on fly balls. Station #3 will work on hitting. Each group will work for five minutes then rotate to the next station.

Station #1 - Partner up and get 10 feet apart while facing each other. The player farthest away will receive a ball being rolled to him **without** using a glove. Make sure his feet are more than shoulder-width apart, his knees are bent, his rear-end is close to the ground (make sure he isn't bending at the waist) and the back of his glove hand is reaching out in front of him near the ground (it is much easier to field a ground ball from the ground up rather than from the top down). The other player should roll a ball to the fielder (seven times) while he is in this proper fielding position (and, he should never stand up...this becomes a good workout, too). The throwing hand acts like the top of an alligator's mouth and closes straight down on his glove hand as if he were eating the ball. Once he fields the ball he throws it back to his partner until he fields seven in a row. After that, he rolls the ball to the other player who should be in the proper fielding position to field seven in a row.

After they begin building the right technique - and, muscle memory - have them put their gloves on, increase to about 20 feet and repeat this drill. Really focus on staying low, hands out front and moving to the ball. After they do the 20-foot roll, have the four players make a 10' x 10' square. Grab one ball, have the first player step with the same foot as his throwing arm while underarm-tossing the ball to the player to his left. Make sure he steps and tosses at the same time while keeping his throwing hand just above his head after he releases the ball until the next player catches it. The ball should continue moving around this square.

These **simple** drills will help hand-eye coordination, proper footwork and build confidence. A baseball player always plays better when he has confidence. These three drills should last five minutes...keep them moving and you will keep their attention.

Station #2 - Partner up in the outfield about 30 feet apart. Have each player throw a lazy fly ball to his buddy. The player catching it should work hard to be under the ball and catch it with both hands above his head. The player throwing the ball should work on stepping and following-through to his target. Do this 10 times for each player.

Next, stay at 30 feet apart from each other. The player throwing the ball has a goal of making it bounce only one time to the other player. The player catching the ball should be in a good fielding position like was mentioned in Station #1. The goal here is to step and throw the ball like a line-drive and making it bounce once before the other player fields it. This will help train the players to keep the ball from being thrown far over someone's head. This will also help the fielder keep the ball in front of him which needs to be a goal for all outfielders. These two drills will also take five minutes.

Station #3 - Have each player grab a bat and spread out to create enough distance between them so they don't hit each other when they swing. Sounds silly, but I have seen players of all ages swing and hit someone because they weren't paying attention. Now, make sure everyone has the proper grip (right-handed batters have the left hand below the right), their middle knuckles (the ones you would knock on wood for good luck) are lined up and a good comfortable, athletic stance that allows both eyes to be facing the pitcher. A coach should stand about 25 feet from the players, wind up like a pitcher and pretend to throw a ball. Ask the batters to work really hard to visualize the ball coming in and then take a good swing at it. Do this 7-10 times so they get their muscles loose.

Now, go to home plate and have one batter stand in the batter's box. Put a sweatshirt just behind his heels. The coach will stand on the pitcher's mound and pretend to throw a pitch. Have the batter swing at the "ball" then drop the bat on the sweatshirt and sprint to first base while never taking his eyes off the base. After he runs straight through first base the next batter is up. Do this drill until your five minutes are almost up and then finish with the batter having fun with a homerun trot around all the bases. The first time you do this you will notice the other groups peeking in and getting excited to come to this station! These two drills - while not actually hitting a ball - develop the proper skills and visualization every batter - at every age - needs to succeed. The sweatshirt drill also trains the batter to never throw the bat.

Now, after the five minutes are up, have each group sprint to another station and do those drills for another five minutes. Do this through all three stations and in 15 minutes, you have simply and effectively covered everything this age group needs to exceed in all aspects of baseball. The outfield drills will actually help your pitchers and catchers as they are developing the same skills they need by throwing to a target and catching the ball.

5- You are only 35 minutes into practice and you have covered a lot. Great work, Coach! It is now time to take some live infield and outfield. This is a good time with the older players in this age group to get some pitching in on the side. If you do this, have them throw 15-25 pitches (increase as the season goes on even though you will probably have less practice time) with the one goal of throwing the ball over the plate for a strike. You will be able to have some pitchers visualize the pitch crossing the plate before they throw it. When they start to understand visualization (I've seen 5 year olds get it) you will see amazing and positive changes. They cant get there without practicing. It's just like riding a bike for the first time. Once they know they can do it they take it to a whole new level.

Place your players in positions in the field where you feel they will succeed the most. If you don't know where that may be (and, it changes as players develop different skills) then ask them to go where they want to play. It doesn't hurt to learn all positions. Now, hit a fly ball to each outfielder and have them throw it to second base. The second baseman will cover second on every ball to the leftfield side of the base (imagine a line dividing the field in two from home plate all the way to the centerfield fence). The shortstop will cover second base on every ball to the rightfield side of the base. After you hit one fly ball to each outfielder then hit one grounder to each of them and have them throw to second base again. By doing the drills in the first two stations they will be ready to start putting it together. Next, do the same thing with one fly ball and one ground ball and have them throw to third base and one more time with them throwing it to the catcher at home plate. Be sure the entire team is communicating to each other by yelling which base they are supposed to throw it ("Take it to second! Take it to third! Send it home!") and encouraging all of their teammates. When the outfielders are done they should sprint in, put on a helmet, grab a bat and swing to get loose and ready to hit.

It is now time for the infield to get its work in. Have all the players stand just inside the baseline in front of their position and on the edge of the grass. The catcher should stand in front of the plate and throw one time to each player. For example, the catcher throws to the third baseman and he throws it back to the catcher. Then, the catcher throws to the shortstop and he throws it back. Continue this all the way around to all the infield positions.

Now, for this age group, the majority of plays they will make will be throwing it to first base. So, remind them to be in their ready position, low to the ground and their hands reaching out for the ball. Hit a grounder to third and have him throw it to first base. Next, do the same with the shortstop, second baseman and first baseman (he should tag first base on his own). Each time before you hit the ball be sure to say, "One out at a time...the play is at first." Within no time the team will be saying it on their own! This is when you know you have opened the door to their baseball brain.

During a real game, ground balls won't always be directly at the fielder. So, after the first round of ground balls and throwing to first, hit the grounder during the second round to each fielder's left so they have to move their feet to get to the ball. Keep saying, "One out at a time...the play is at first." The next time around the infield hit the ball to the infielder's right side and the final round hit a slow roller so they have to charge the ball quickly.

Very rarely in this age group do you see double plays like you do at the higher levels so try not to complicate the game and spend too much time on that. At this age, most plays are caught fly balls and ground balls being thrown to first. Focus on what will get you three outs the quickest so your team can get up to bat and score some runs!

LIVE SITUATIONS

The outfield and infield session should take about 10 minutes so now you are left with 10-15 minutes in practice. This is the time you should spend going over situations your team will have in their games. If you have 12 players, then put players at each position except for pitcher (where a coach should be the pitcher for this drill and step in at catcher if there is a play at the plate) and catcher. This will leave five batters and runners. Everyone wants to hit so be prepared for some to whine a little bit when you put them in the field. If this happens try saying, "I understand you want to hit and if you keep working hard on defense I will give you that chance." Then, do your best to end the conversation at that. Over time, the player will trust you and your words and will recognize that you give everyone equal chances.

For this drill, put a batting tee on the plate and have the hitters hit off of that. Professionals use a batting tee and your team should, too. Plus, it will keep things moving and less standing around. The first batter should hit the ball, drop the bat (feel free to keep the sweatshirt at his heels) and sprint to first. Your job as the pitcher/coach during this drill is to just pay attention to what happens when the ball is in play. Before each batter hits remind them, "One out at a time." Let the first five get one at-bat, run the bases if they don't get out and keep your notebook close to make notes on situations to talk about after practice.

After the first five hit, rotate them to the field and let the others get their chance to hit and run. Do this until everyone has hit at least one time off of the tee. This will take you pretty close to your one hour of practice time. Before the practice is over, split your team evenly and have them stand in front of both dugouts (six on one side and six on the other side). This is where you should teach them to meet by home plate and shake hands, or high five or fist bump. When this is done ask them to sprint to the one of the outfield lines and take a knee. Now is the time you quickly talk about what they accomplished in practice and how they are better baseball players than they were just one hour ago! Wait until you see the smiles and you will know you did a great job. Remind them to help clean up all the gear, grab their bags and ask them to thank their parents for allowing them a chance to play baseball.

FOR THE BULLPEN IN YOUR BRAIN: Great job, Coach! You just simplified the game of baseball to what it is really about...running, catching, throwing, fielding, hitting, sportsmanship and having fun. You stayed on time (which always makes the parents happy) and your team improved. The next step will define you as a coach. Once you see that everyone has a ride home, knows when the next practice or game is and the field looks as good as when you arrived...you need to make notes in your notebook for each player and his IBP. This will help you continue defining each player's IBP so you can help each one improve the next time you are together. Be sure to make a note of who got to hit first and even plan for who gets to hit first the next time. This should take you 5-15 minutes (while it is still fresh in your mind) and you have nearly written the plan for the next practice without taking more time out of your day.

If you can try to incorporate the same stations at every practice, modify them as needed, then your players will know what to expect. Remember to take notes during games on situations your team needs to work on and recreate those situations in the next practice. This guarantees your players are meeting your definition of success.

Eventually, you can start having live batting practice with live situations. For example, remind them that getting the first out before a runner gets on base is your first goal. Then, it is **one out at a time**. The quicker you get three outs the quicker you get to hit! Until they play on a more competitive team, it really doesn't matter how they get the outs! When you can get this message across to your players you will have quick, effective practices that don't linger on and on and on.

"It gets late early out there." - Yogi Berra

PRACTICE SCHEDULE:
PLAYERS 11-14 YEARS OLD

Perhaps you skipped the Practice Schedule section for the players who are 5-10 but the following information is important for all ages. There are some baseball etiquettes and superstitions to talk about for all players before the team steps on the field. The earlier these can be taught the more the Baseball Gods will shine on you and your team! First of all, never - absolutely never - step on the chalk when you're running on or off the field...in practice and in games. Watch the professionals, they will sometimes jump over the chalk lines! This is the chalk down each infield line and both outfield lines. Bad luck may visit your team if you do touch the chalk and it is not worth the risk. Next, at the beginning of practice or before a game, never warm up on the infield. Always run and throw in the outfield closest to your dugout. Finally, when a baseball player steps on the field he needs to be taught that it is his time to forget about everything going on in his personal life and just focus on **simply** having fun and **simply** playing a game.

1 - 1/2 HOUR PRACTICE SCHEDULE

If you are coaching this age group it has naturally become a little more competitive. Some leagues will have All-Star teams or travel teams. However, no matter how good the players are you still must keep the game **simple** and focus on fundamentals.

1- If you are using the first base dugout during practice, jog to the right field corner then stay along the outfield fence and jog to the left field corner and then jog back together as a team. Do this three times to get the blood flowing. As was mentioned earlier, stretching cold muscles increases a chance of injury so get a little sweat going first and warm up those muscles before you stretch. (3-5 minutes)

2- Have the team get together along the right field line, in a circle (or have three players lead the team and have lines of players facing them), and then go through a series of leg stretches, back stretches and arm stretches (arm circles going forward then backward starting small and getting bigger are great for this). Finish with 21 crunches (Roberto Clemente wore #21 and it can't hurt you to honor him!). (5 minutes)

3- Ask the players if anybody has a sore arm. If they do, be smart about this to avoid further injury. Partner up, get on a knee (right handers on their right knee with the left knee at a right angle and the kneecap pointing toward their partner and left handers on their left knee with the right knee at a right angle and the kneecap point toward their target) and lightly throw to start getting loose. After they make the throw, make sure their throwing arm stays over their other knee on the follow-through and stretch even more. After two minutes of this stand up and increase the throwing distance. As well as getting loose, be sure the players are throwing using a 4 seam grip. Again, this means the "horseshoe" of the baseball should be perpendicular to the players' fingers. Throwing with all 4 seams will keep the ball moving straight. The earlier a player can learn to grip the ball this way will help him tremendously throughout his playing days. Holding a ball with 2 seams (the "horseshoe" of the ball will be above his fingertips) will cause the ball to move more and not go as fast. Continue increasing the distance to make their arms stronger. Incorporate some long-toss to strengthen and stretch their arms. Keep in mind that the ball does not need to be thrown on a line...rather, crow-hop (get the body moving forward) and let your body take over how to throw the ball with the right height and angle to get to your partner. (10-15 minutes)

4- Most of the teams in this age bracket also have 12 players so now get into three groups of four players. Adjust accordingly based on how many players but try to keep even numbers so everyone has a partner. Station #1 will work on ground balls and double plays. Station #2 will work on fly balls and relays. Station #3 will work on hitting and bunting. Each group will work for 10 minutes then rotate to the next station.

Station #1 - Partner up and get 10 feet apart while facing each other. The player farthest away will receive a ball being rolled to him **without** using a glove. Make sure his feet are more than shoulder-width apart, his knees are bent, his rear-end is close to the ground (make sure he isn't bending at the waist) and the back of his glove hand is reaching out in front of him near the ground (it is much easier to field a ground ball from the ground up rather than from the top down). Even though younger players do this drill it is important to incorporate at this age, too. Remind your players the professionals do this drill, too. The other player should roll a ball to the fielder (seven times) while he is in this proper fielding position (and, the fielder should never stand up...this becomes a good workout, too). The throwing hand acts like the top of an alligator's mouth and closes straight down on his glove hand as if he were eating the ball. Once he fields the ball he throws it back to his partner until he fields seven in a row. After that, he rolls the ball to the other player who should be in the proper fielding position to field seven in a row. After they begin building the right technique - and muscle memory - have them put their gloves on, increase to about 20 feet and repeat this drill while throwing the ball a little bit harder than the 10-foot drill. Really focus on staying low, hands out front and moving to the ball.

The following drill is one of my favorites. I played shortstop and second base and this helped me develop the proper footwork and skills to become my very best at turning a double play. Even though I did this drill as a player in the '70s and '80s I still use it today as a coach. Have the four players make a 15' x 15' square and face the player to their right. Grab one ball, have the first player shuffle then step with the same foot as his throwing arm while underhand-tossing the ball to the player to his left. Keep it **simple** by making sure he shuffles (it's important to get the body moving toward the target) then steps and tosses at the same time while keeping his throwing hand just above his head after he releases the ball until the next player catches it. The player catching the ball should step to the ball with the same foot as his glove hand as he is catching it. Visually, this should look like a string is attached from his glove to his foot and the two should move together. The players should move to the next spot in the square after they toss the ball.

Now, after one minute of this drill, stay in the square and reverse the way the ball is going. The goal here is to catch the ball then quickly and accurately "push" it to the next guy. By a "push" the right elbow should be pointed at the target and the push simply means the hand and ball extend to the target while shuffling then stepping with the right foot and holding the release until the next player catches it (switch this for any lefties you may have). There is no throwing or underarm tossing...just a push release. To show this, you can make a fist with your right hand and put it thumb-side on the center of your chest with your elbow pointed out and parallel to the ground (almost as if you had your hand on your heart for The National Anthem). Now, just bend your elbow and extend your arm. This is the "push."

Do this for two minutes and have the players follow the ball to the next spot in the square.

Next, take your players to second base, or use something to simulate a base and put two players at shortstop and two at second base so they can work on a double play. As players develop, they will react to what is most comfortable for them but this is where you can help build their foundation. Let's start with a double play from the third baseman or shortstop tossing to the second baseman (in this drill we will just use the shortstop). As the ground ball goes to the shortstop the second baseman should sprint and get his left foot on the base, give the shortstop a target and be balanced in an athletic position. Roll a ball to the shortstop, he will field it and underhand-toss it to the second baseman. This is the same motion your players did in the first part of the square drill. Now you are **simply** taking it to a new level. After the second baseman catches the toss, he should plant on his right foot, step with his left foot toward first base and throw to a coach (who does not have to be as far away as first base) or, if there's not another coach, then simulate throwing to first.

After each player gets 10 reps of this drill at each position, switch the double play and roll the ball to the second baseman who will now "push" it to the shortstop. As the ball is being rolled, the shortstop should sprint to second base, plant his right foot on the base, give a target and be in an athletic position to make the play. As the ball is in the air from the second baseman the shortstop should step with his left foot toward the ball while dragging the right foot across the base and then throw to first base. You have now simply and effectively taught the proper way to turn a double play. Great job, Coach!

Station #2 - Have your players make a long, straight line covering most of the outfield. Hit or throw a fly ball to the player farthest away (so it should be players 1-2-3-4 in a line and the coach will be next to player 1). Player 4 should be sure to catch the fly ball above his head with both hands (the throwing hand should be just behind the pocket of the glove and available as a backup in case the ball pops out of the glove). As soon as he catches the ball, the other three players should have their hands up and providing a great target. Player 4, who caught the ball, should shuffle or crow-hop (a quick shuffle jump to use his legs and get more velocity on the ball as his weight moves forward) and throw to player 3 who will then throw to player 2 and then to player 1. Players 1, 2 and 3 should be facing the player who is throwing to them and here is something you **simply need to coach**...as the ball is being thrown to them, the player catching it needs to turn (by dropping his glove-hand foot back) and as soon as he catches the ball he will already be in a position to throw it to the next player. If he catches the ball and *then* turns it will be too slow to throw out a potential runner in a real game. It's the simple things like this that can make a difference in a game. After player 4 throws the ball he should sprint to where player 1 is and then each player moves up a spot. Do this drill so each player gets five chances to catch a fly ball and make accurate throws with good footwork.

The next outfield drill will teach players to catch a ball on the run while communicating to each other. Place a player in left field and one in centerfield. You will stand just behind where the shortstop would be in a game. Throw a ball (mix in fly balls with ground balls) between the two so they have to run for it. Be sure you talk to them about communicating who has the ball so they do not run into each other and get hurt. We teach saying loudly, "Ball...ball...ball" by the player who will catch it. The other player will then acknowledge by saying, "You...you...you" and then get out of the way by sprinting to the outfield fence side of the player who will catch it (this puts him in position to help if the ball is missed). This drill will help all of your players be on the same communication page with each other no matter what position they play in a game. This drill is incredibly important so spend the remaining time on it until you rotate stations.

Station #3 - Have each player grab a bat and spread out to create enough distance between them so they don't hit each other when they swing. Sounds silly, but I have seen players of all ages swing and hit someone because they weren't paying attention. Now, make sure everyone has the proper grip (right-handed batters have the left hand below the right), their middle knuckles (the ones you would knock on wood for good luck) are lined up and a good comfortable, athletic stance that allows both eyes to be facing the pitcher. A coach should stand about 25 feet from the players, wind up like a pitcher and pretend to throw a ball. Ask the batters to work really hard visualizing the ball coming in, taking a good swing at it, visualizing the ball hitting the bat while keeping the head down the bat's barrel and focusing on "putting the ball in play." Do this 7-10 times so they get their muscles loose and their brains working hard to visualize.

Now, somewhat of a lost art in baseball is the bunt. Most players - and a few coaches - just love the homerun and hope to win games by waiting for the long ball. However, the bunt can be even more effective. A good bunt can change the momentum of the game as much - if not more - than a homerun. And, your entire team can bunt while very few can hit a homerun. It is a **simple** strategy! A good bunt - and sometimes just showing a bunt - can ruin the rhythm of a good pitcher. Instantly, the pitcher and all the infielders have to be on their toes. Once you can get the defense thinking...they will tense up and this is your opportunity to create opportunities for your team. This is strategic coaching at its best. Play the percentages and make things happen!

The coach in this drill should stand in front of the pitcher's mound and be sure you have a few baseballs. Have a batter at the plate, pitch to him and have him make three sacrifice bunts by "catching the ball with the bat." The player's only goal here is to get the ball on the ground and avoid bunting it directly back at the pitcher. Remind the batter that he just needs to sacrifice his out by advancing his teammate either to second or third base with the bunt. Remind your players the definition of success and do everything for your team. You should teach the concept that the batter squares his body and shoulders to the pitcher and gets in his bunting stance (the bat is out front facing the pitcher with the barrel slightly above the handle, eye level, fingers behind the bat) *before* the pitcher throws the ball. It is okay to show the defense you are bunting in this situation.

STRATEGIC COACHING: In fact, as a coach, make note of how the defense reacts. You may notice their third baseman always charges on the bunt. If this is the case, and if you have a runner on second base, you could call a fake bunt and a steal. Your runner will take third while your batter shows bunt and the third baseman is running in. In this situation, the defense has nobody covering third even if their shortstop tries to get there in time. This is a great way to advance your runners on a fake bunt. Okay, back to the drill...after all your batters succeed on their third sacrifice bunt, have them sprint to first base after **simply** bunting the ball on the ground.

When all of the batters have successfully bunted three sacrifices now have them bunt for a hit. The key here is to <u>not</u> show the bunt as early as you would in a sacrifice situation and to catch the defense on their heels. The two spots to bunt for hits are down the third base line and past the pitcher between first and second base (more of a push bunt). Have your batters bunt two down the line and one between first and second and on the third bunt have them sprint through first base.

We teach the "pop-pop bunt for hit" technique. For a right-handed batter, this means instead of squaring up to the pitcher as we would for a sacrifice, after the pitcher releases the ball the batter drops his right foot back a few inches (almost like a sprinter would start a race) then pushes off his back foot at the same time he bunts the ball. The "pop-pop" is really "right foot drop, left foot forward" very quickly.

Right. Left. Pop. Pop. This helps start his running momentum when he bunts down the third base line and this also helps push the ball between first and second if he is trying to place the bunt past the pitcher. A left-handed batter will start his momentum by crossing his left foot over the right as he catches the ball with the bat. The right hand will guide the direction of the bunt either down third or dragging the ball between first and second base.

Bunting not only creates opportunities for your offense but it forces the batter to see the ball all the way to the bat without pulling his head (which sometimes happens to batters when they swing). Hitters have slumps in Little League all the way through Major League. That is the nature of baseball. Remember, baseball needs time to balance itself. One way to avoid a long slump is to have the batter bunt, bunt and bunt as much as he can in practice. By seeing the ball make contact with the bat in a bunting situation, the batter's brain is being reminded he must always see the ball in every situation...bunting or swinging. Bunting can be the magical "slump-buster." Great bunters are also great hitters. It is a **simple** formula!

5- You have about 35 minutes left in practice, you have covered a lot, helped your team improve and it is time to see the hard work pay off. It is now time to take some live infield and outfield and have your pitchers get some repetitions on the mound.

Let's start with the pitchers and keep it **simple** to maximize their potential. The number one goal at any age is to throw strikes. Having your pitchers **simply** work on the side of the field - with a goal - will increase their confidence and they will be ready to carry that confidence to the field. Have two of your pitchers (rotate which two get to pitch each practice) and one catcher (in full gear) grab three baseballs and go to the bullpen (if you don't have a bullpen or practice mound then walk-off the correct distance from the pitcher's mound to the plate and make this your bullpen). Use a Sharpie and mark one of the baseballs with your team logo or color it in...this will be your "money ball." Have the first pitcher get loose with the catcher and be sure to do this with a purpose. This means, even though he is just warming up, the catcher will give a different target location with his glove each warm-up pitch. This is <u>simply</u> taking practice with a purpose to a new level. Once the pitcher is loose he will throw 15 fastballs to the catcher. The second pitcher will keep track of the pitches and how many of them are thrown for strikes. Every fifth pitch, have your player throw it with the "money ball." If the pitcher throws a strike with the "money ball" it counts as an automatic out against the first batter of an inning. Remember, if the first batter of an inning gets on base, he will score nearly 90% of the time. This drill will teach your pitchers to focus ("Ag-Ack") on getting that first out and increasing your team's chances of not giving up a run. It is a fun and competitive drill that will be recalled in your pitcher's memory whenever he takes the mound in a game. After he throws his 15 pitches, the next pitcher will throw and do the same drill.

While the pitchers are throwing the rest of the team should be at their positions in the field. However, before they take the field, have them get in a huddle by the dugout, put their hands in the middle and on the count of three say, "Team." Then, they should sprint to their positions instead of taking the field walking or casually jogging. Now, hit a fly ball to each outfielder and have them throw it to second base. The second baseman will cover second on every ball to the leftfield side of the base (imagine a line dividing the field in two from home plate all the way to the centerfield fence). The shortstop will cover second base on every ball to the rightfield side of the base. After you hit one fly ball to each outfielder then hit one grounder to each of them and have them throw to second base again. By doing the drills in the first two stations they will be ready to start putting it all together. Next, do the same thing with one fly ball and one ground ball and have them throw to third base and one more time with them throwing it to the catcher at home plate. Be sure the entire team is communicating to each other by yelling which base they are supposed to throw it ("Take it to second! Take it to third! Send it home!") and encouraging all of their teammates. When the outfielders are done they should sprint to your dugout (or, in front of it) and support the infielders while they take their ground balls.

It is now time for the infield to get its work in. Have all the players stand just inside the baseline in front of their position and on the edge of the grass. The catcher should stand in front of the plate and throw one time to each player. For example, the catcher throws to the third baseman and he throws it back to the catcher. Then, the catcher throws to the shortstop and he throws it back. Continue this all the way around the infield positions.

Now, for this age group, batters will be all different sizes and speeds as their bodies develop during their growth spurts. So, remind your infielders to be in their ready position, low to the ground and their hands reaching out for the ball. Hit a grounder to third and have him throw it to first base. Next, do the same with the shortstop, second baseman and first baseman (he should tag first base on his own). Each time before you hit the ball be sure to say, "One out at a time...the play is at first." Within no time the team will be saying it on their own! This is when you know you have opened the door to their baseball brain.

As we talked about in the 5-10 practice guide, ground balls won't always be directly at the fielder in games. It is important to simulate what may happen in games instead of practicing the perfect grounder right at the player. So, after the first round of ground balls and throwing to first, hit the grounder during the second round to each fielder's left so they have to move their feet to get to the ball. Keep saying, "One out at a time...the play is at first." The next time around the infield hit the ball to the infielder's right side and the final round hit a slow roller so they have to charge the ball quickly. At all ages, most plays in a game are caught fly balls and ground balls being thrown to first. Focus on what will get you three outs the quickest so your team can get up to bat and score some runs!

Teams you play at this level will start stealing and bunting more than they do in the earlier ages and it is important to have your defense prepared for these situations as well as the plays at first base. So now you can quickly work on the bunt. As the coach hitting the infield, square around as if you were making a sacrifice bunt and be sure everyone on the team recognizes what you are doing by yelling, "Bunt!" In **simple** bunt coverage, the first and third basemen should come charging in while the second baseman sprints over to cover first base. Your shortstop can either cover second base or sprint to cover third base (usually done if there is a runner at second). Roll the ball to the third baseman charging and have him throw it to first. Then, square around again, be sure they all recognize the bunt and roll the ball to the first baseman and have him throw to first after he fields the bunt. On the third bunt, place it just in front of the plate and have the catcher make the play. The catcher should get the ball with his bare hand, step inside the field and throw. This will give him a better angle to first base so he takes away the risk of hitting the runner who bunted the ball.

Now that you have covered bunt situations you should quickly and simply cover steal situations. I like to have the catcher in a position as if he were receiving the pitch. Be sure his rear is up in the air a little bit so he can catch the pitch, step and throw nearly in one motion. Stand in front of the mound, tell your team there is a runner on first and throw to the catcher. The team should yell, "Runner!" This is a good habit to get into so the catcher knows the runner is stealing. The catcher should throw to second base. Have your middle infielders alternate who is catching the throw and putting the tag on the runner while the other is in position to backup a poor throw and keep it from getting into centerfield. Do this twice to second base and twice to third base. Pay attention to everyone involved in this and make a note if you need to work on this in more detail. If you do, incorporate this drill into one of your stations at the next practice.

So far you have covered plays at first base, bunts and steals plus your pitchers are getting work in the bullpen. Now, it is time to turn double plays. In your first station earlier in practice you covered the fundamentals of the double play. Remind your players what to do and then see how they perform. Remind them, "Runner on first, let's turn a double play and make sure of one out no matter what." This is a reminder that if the fielder bobbles the ground ball then just make the play at first base rather than trying to make it at second which is unlikely because the grounder wasn't fielded cleanly. Hit each player a grounder and watch them make the double play!

Now, finish your infield session with one more ground ball and have them either throw out the runner at the plate or one more time at first base. Again, this is where you need to make great notes in your notebook. Most ground ball plays - at any level - tend to be completed at first base so check your notes and see what you need to work on to be the best your team can be. Preparation and positive attitudes are the unsung heroes in baseball! The infield and outfield work should take no more than 10-15 minutes and you **simply** created nearly every situation your team will come across in a game. Nice work!

LIVE SITUATIONS

A fun and great game to play the remainder of practice is "Work Up." This game will create game situations and it will tie together everything you have worked on in practice. You will need a player at every position except pitcher and catcher. So, you will have seven players in the field and the rest will be batters. Place one of the batters at second base to start this drill and explain to your batters that their job is to move that runner to third base either by bunting or hitting a ground ball to first or second base. The coach will pitch as if it were a real game and every ball hit is a live ball and the defense must make the play.

Here is where it gets fun and becomes a learning situation. If the batter hits a fly ball and it is caught by the defense then the batter goes to the position where the ball is caught and that fielder gets to go hit. So, if the batter hits a fly ball to centerfield and the centerfielder catches it...the batter must grab his glove and hat and sprint to center while the centerfielder sprints in and stands in line waiting for his turn to hit. If the batter hits a ground ball and the defense successfully makes the play to get an out at first base then everyone rotates one position. This means the rightfielder moves over to center, center goes to left, left goes to third base, third goes to shortstop, short goes to second base and first gets to go hit. The batter who grounded out must hustle to play right field. If the batter gets a hit then he gets to stay on base and he will get to hit again after he scores. If there is a runner on first base and the batter hits a grounder to shortstop and the runner at first is forced out at second base then nobody gets to rotate. This will keep game situations active. Keep track of outs and clear any runners after three outs...but those runners get to keep hitting until they ground or fly out. Since all of your players will probably play a different position during this game...you will learn who can play what positions the best.

In 90 minutes you certainly have covered a lot and kept your team enthused. Before you send your players on their way, be sure to meet with them, briefly cover what they learned and why, then remind them they are responsible for getting the gear together and cleaning the field and dugout for the next team. Have them shake hands with each other and praise them for working hard.

FOR THE BULLPEN IN YOUR BRAIN: Great job, Coach! You just directed a productive practice, your players are better than they were when they arrived and you were able to discover what your team can do well and what skills need more attention. Before you head home or back to work, spend 5-15 minutes writing in your notebook about what you covered in practice, assessing your players' IBPs and what you want to cover the next time you step on the diamond. If you get in a habit of doing this while all your thoughts are fresh you will be rewarded with more time for yourself. Fight the temptation to just take ground balls and batting practice because you see that is what other teams are doing. You will have those practices, too. However, if you only take ground balls, fly balls and batting practice your players will be bored quickly, they will not perform well in games and you run the risk of losing your enthusiasm as a coach. Remember, your team's job on defense is to get three outs as quickly as possible so they can get a chance to hit. Your team's job on offense is to put the ball in play to create more opportunities to score runs. It really is a **simple** game. You can simplify it more for your players by practicing actual situations they will have in games. Batting practice isn't what happens in a game so fight the temptation to spend too much time on it in practice. The only time batting practice happens in games is when your team isn't prepared to make three outs as quickly - and, **simply** - as possible.

"Victory or defeat is not determined at the moment of crisis, but rather in the long and unspectacular period of preparation."
- Anonymous

PRACTICE SCHEDULE:
PLAYERS 15-19 YEARS OLD

High school baseball players and American Legion players are fun to coach. They are really starting to understand their identity. They are developing habits (mostly good) to help succeed in school and on the field. Their learning curves are much shorter than when they were younger. And, they are learning to be accountable and understanding of the fact that if they work hard...good things will happen. If they don't work hard, they may get left in the dust by someone who is putting in the time and effort.

Designing practice for this age is fun because you can really design it around each player's IBP. It is important to keep working on the fundamentals but now you can ask these players to do more work on their own at home and see the rewards quicker. You will also be able to define each player's role and help them develop their strengths. There will be some players who simply can't hit a 80mph or 90mph fastball. No worries! Work on their bunting skills and they can still be a key part of your team.

2-HOUR PRACTICE SCHEDULE

One of the best parts of coaching this level is you can have multiple stations and the players will know - for the most part - what to do. You can then spend a lot of time observing, stepping in to fine-tune things, and when you establish the team's goals the players will run the drills in practice allowing you more flexibility in where you need to be.

1- Make a rule that the players arrive dressed and ready to practice. The dugout isn't a changing room and it is your job to teach your team how to respect the game of baseball. This also means that arriving on time is too late. Making the players arrive early will help them in the game of life.

2- As soon as practice begins have the players go to the nearest outfield line and start getting loose. I have my players work on their leadoffs, secondary leads, steals and delayed steals right away. They are not to talk to each other while they do this. This is "Ag-Ack" time. This is a great way to get loose before stretching. If you have ever been to Spring Training or a MLB game...you will see the professionals get loose this way, too. Your players are getting two things done at once...getting loose and fine-tuning their base running skills. After seven minutes of this, the team should get together and jog to the centerfield wall and back two times. (7-10 minutes)

3- Stretch as a team. Have your captains lead this stretch. If you don't have captains then be sure to alternate who leads stretching so everyone has a chance. (5-10 minutes)

4- Partner up and begin to throw starting with throwing on a knee first. Middle infielders should throw with each other. Corner infielders should throw with each other. Outfielders should throw with each other and your battery (pitchers and catchers) should throw with each other. Throw on a knee for 3-5 minutes before standing up and increasing the distance. Keep increasing the distance every seven throws and spend some time long-tossing to strengthen the arms. The infielders should finish with quick-toss from about 15 feet (working on their hand speed by getting the ball out of the glove and throwing it as quickly and accurately as possible). (10-15 minutes)

After warming up, have the outfielders and catchers go hit (**5A**)while the infielders (**5B**) work on infield drills with the pitchers.

5A- If you have the resources, try to have four hitting stations. Bunting, batting tee, soft-toss and situational hitting in the cage. The bunting station can have up to four players, one bunts while the other three throw to him. Have this group bunt a series of sacrifices, bunt for hits and squeeze bunts. The batting tee station should work on inside, middle and outside pitches. The players should hit five at each location and then alternate. The soft-toss should work on bat speed with a series of five tosses. The key to this drill is the player tossing the balls should toss them in a rapid-fire, yet controlled tempo. And the work in the batting cage will tie all of the situations together. Start with two sacrifice bunts, two bunts for hits and two squeeze bunts. Follow this with three hit and runs, three ground balls to the right side (to move the runner at second base) and three free swings before rotating with the other player who is throwing the pitches from behind the L-Screen. The next time through in the cage will be five two-strike hits (have the batter widen his stance and start his swing with his hands near his sternum) focusing on putting the ball in play and then five free swings. All stations should keep working until the players in the cage are done with their reps. Then, everyone rotates to the next station.

When all four stations have had their rotations they will have had at least 75-100 swings and situations in a matter of 30 minutes. This is much more effective than standing around and hitting without a purpose.

5B- While the outfielders are hitting at their stations, the infielders and pitchers are working on footwork, hand-eye drills and situational repetitions. Have everyone partner with a teammate and work on short-hops with each other. The key here is to extend the glove to the ball trying to eliminate bad hops. Stand 10-15 feet apart, both players low to the ground, knees bent and in a ready position. Time this for 60 seconds as they throw short-hops to each other. After 60 seconds, work on fielding back-hand grounders. There really is no fundamentally correct way to do this other than being sure the glove-hand is reaching and extended out front. If the fielder is not extending his glove and fields the ball behind his head he is far less-likely to make a play. Do this drill for 60 seconds. Repeat both these drills one more time. (4-5 minutes)

Now, get two cones (or helmets) and place the first one 10 steps before second base and place the next cone 15 steps before second base. Have your first baseman and pitchers rotate at first base and the rest of the infielders should be between second base and the first cone. Roll a ball to the fielder near the first cone, he must field the ball while staying low to the ground with his hands out front. After he fields the ground ball, he should stay low and shuffle towards first base until he is near the second cone and then make a good throw while his momentum carries him to his target. This teaches proper fielding and footwork. Stay low, see the ball into the glove and keep staying low while getting the body moving at your target. The first baseman should start in an athletic position, giving the fielder a great target and then stepping/reaching to the ball while it is in the air. The glove-hand foot should be in sync with the glove as if they were tied together with a string when they stretch to the ball. The other foot should have its heel on the base. Do this drill for five minutes while always moving and working hard. (5 minutes)

COACHING HINT: If your first baseman is having troubles making plays...check his footwork first. Often times, first basemen get in a habit of stepping *before* the ball is being thrown to them and then they get stuck if the ball is not thrown exactly at their glove. If this is the case, remind them to step to the ball when it is in the air as if their glove had a string tied to the toe of their cleat.

After the footwork drill, have the middle infielders turn double plays while your corners (first and third basemen) and pitchers work on bunt coverages.

Your shortstop and second baseman need to have a relationship that has no weaknesses. They need to feed off of each other's energy, know each other's thoughts and have each other's back all of the time. In this drill, start with rolling a ball to the shortstop and turning a double play. Be sure the second baseman hustles to the bag with his left foot on the base and as he catches the ball he needs to quickly plant on his right foot and drive his momentum back to first base as he throws to complete the double play. Because the other infielders are working on bunt coverages, your middle infielders do not need to throw the ball to first for this drill. Focus on getting the out at second base with perfect footwork. Roll five grounders to the shortstop and then switch and roll five grounders to the second baseman. When the shortstop is turning the double play, he needs to have his right foot on second base and step with his left foot to the ball while dragging his right across the bag. When this relationship between the two middle infielders "clicks" the timing of their double plays will be perfect. As with any relationship...this takes time and hard work!

As the middle infielders are working on double plays your other infielders should work on defending the bunt. We teach three different bunt coverages based on the situation. The first coverage is an all-out blitz to be sure we get an out. Usually this is with a good lead and/or the other team is near the bottom of their lineup. You want to prevent a big inning by getting one guaranteed out. In this coverage, the third and first basemen come charging in and protect their lines while the pitcher covers the bunt right back at him. While they are charging the second baseman sprints and covers first base. In this drill, since the second baseman is working on double plays at the same time, have one of your first basemen cover first while the other charges. The next bunt coverage has the third baseman charging, the pitcher covering the first base line and the first baseman staying at first base. This is a good coverage with a slow runner on first who you may be able to throw out at second base. Whatever you call this coverage be sure the second baseman covers second and the shortstop wheels over and covers third base. The final bunt coverage keeps the third baseman at third, the pitcher will then cover the third base line and the first baseman charges in and covers his line. The second baseman will cover first and the shortstop will cover second. This is when there is a runner at second and you want to try to get him out at third.

Some teams use numbers for each of their coverages. For example, 1-3-1 may be the first. 2-3-2 may be the second and 3-1-3 may be the third. Naming this is entirely up to you. We call our all-out blitz coverage our mascot's name. We use any state (Colorado, Florida, etc) for our second coverage and we use any player's last name for the final coverage. Come up with some simple names that your team will remember easily but not too simple for other teams to pick up! Do this drill and the double play drill for five minutes.

COACHING HINT: One of my favorite things to do as a coach is steal the other team's signs. I thrive on it and I have our players try to figure them out, too! For those who are not in the first nine, this is a great way to keep them focused during a game. If you know your opponent's bunt coverage, then you can steal and fake bunt at the same time. They will be out of position and this gives you momentum to score more runs. If their third baseman is charging for a bunt and you have a runner on second base....call a steal and fake bunt! Nobody will be covering third base and you just advanced the runner without surrendering an out.

You now have covered a lot of situations and you still have 15 minutes left of work for your infielders and pitchers. This is a great time to take a power infield with lots of ground balls and situations. Have two coaches hitting with empty baseball buckets at each base. You will hit a series of five situations for three minutes each for the next 15 minutes. The series (A-E) are:

A- Coach #1 hits ground balls to third and he will be throwing to first (the first baseman puts the balls he catches in the bucket. At the same time, Coach #2 hits ground balls to the shortstop and he will be throwing to second base and using the bucket at second.

B- Coach #1 hits ground balls to the first baseman and he will throw to third. If you have enough pitchers for this drill, have them cover first and alternate the first baseman flip to the pitcher. The key here is that the pitcher sprints at a 45-degree angle to the first base line and then straight up the line so he can catch the flip on the run, easily get the out and avoid contact with the runner. Coach #2 will hit ground balls to the second baseman who will push the ball to the shortstop covering second base.

C- Coach #1 hits ground balls to the third baseman for the 5-4-3 double play. Coach #2 hits ground balls to the shortstop and he just tosses the balls in the bucket behind second base.

D- Coach #1 hits ground balls to the second baseman for the 4-6-3 double play. Coach #2 hits ground balls to the third baseman and he just tosses the balls in the bucket at third base.

E- Coach #1 hits ground balls to the shortstop for the 6-4-3 double play. Coach #2 lays down hard bunts to the third baseman simulating a squeeze bunt.

COACHING HINT: One important part of defending the squeeze bunt is making sure your third baseman sprints to

home as soon as the runner on third takes off. You will have a better chance of getting the out at home plus your third baseman will be in a position to catch a bad bunt in the air and get a double play.

You are now just a little more than one hour into practice and have covered a lot of situations your players will see in games. At this time, have the infielders and pitchers go hit for the next 30 minutes, using the same four stations that the outfielders and catchers used. The outfielders and catchers will now spend the next half hour on defense.

The outfielders have not thrown much in the last half hour so you don't want to have them going full speed just yet. Start with making a line from home plate all the way to centerfield and spacing about 50 feet apart. The catcher will stay with you as you hit fly balls. Hit a fly to the farthest outfielder in centerfield. After he catches it he will start a relay by throwing to the player closest to him who will then throw it to the next guy until it reaches the catcher. After each player catches and throws the ball he sprints farther out to the next spot. The outfielder in centerfield will sprint all the way to the relay man nearest the catcher. Do this drill for five minutes to get loose.

After the outfielders are loose have them go to their positions in the outfield. The coach should stand between the pitcher's mound and second base with the catcher. If you have an extra catcher, put him at second base to help catch balls being thrown in. Hit a round of fly balls to each outfielder and have them either throw it to the catcher at second base or one-hop it to the catcher with you (this will strengthen their arm and improve their accuracy for when they need to hit the cut-off man). Next, hit a round of line drives to each outfielder followed by a round of ground balls to each player. Repeat this sequence of a fly ball, line drive and ground ball five times. This will take about 10 minutes.

COACHING HINT: If you notice your outfielders are not very accurate with their throws...check their grips. Be sure they are using a four seam grip so the ball doesn't tail so much. They should be crow-hopping and throwing right at their target. Also, make sure they are catching the fly balls above their head and remind them that no line drive or ground ball gets by them...ever!

For the next five minutes, hit fly balls and line drives from home plate and have your outfielders try to one-hop their throws right to the catcher. Be sure to put them in a position to succeed by hitting shallow fly balls and nothing over their heads. There will be a game this year when the tying or winning run is on third base with one out and the batter hits a fly ball. Tell your outfielders this situation and see how they perform. Then, the next situation has the winning run on second base and you hit a line drive and the outfielders have to throw him out at home with a perfect one-hop to the catcher.

COACHING HINT: After an outfielder makes the perfect throw to home, praise him and ask him to lock that in his brain for when that same situation comes up in a game.

After five minutes of throwing to home have the outfielders stand on each base. They are going to help the catchers work on their throws for the next 10 minutes. You will stand about 15 feet in front of the catcher towards the mound. Start with a runner on first and the batter misses a bunt. In this situation, 91% of the time the runner on first is anticipating the ball being bunted and is caught leaning towards second base. A good catcher can throw him out if he has worked on this in practice. Tell your catcher the situation, throw the pitch and have him throw to first without any hesitation. Do this five times.

The next situation has a runner on first who is stealing. As you pitch the ball have the outfielders yell, "Runner" so the catcher knows he is stealing. Throw the runner out at second five times. Now, do the same thing at third base.

COACHING HINT: If you have an extra outfielder, have him stand in the batter's box with a helmet on and a bat so the catcher gets used to a batter being there. Have him stand in both sides of the box. Also, be sure your catcher is wearing all his gear so he gets used to throwing with it on.

For the next three minutes, have each outfielder grab three baseballs and stand halfway between the pitching mound and the plate. They will throw balls in the dirt to the catcher. Remind the catcher that for this situation there is a runner on third base and he can't score on a wild pitch. The catcher needs to turn into a human backstop! This is a fun drill and the results pay off in games.

Finally, to finish this session, have each outfielder stand - one at a time - at the plate and each one of them will throw three pop-ups to the catcher. There are very few coaches who can hit a perfect pop-up to the catcher so this helps make the drill more effective.

COACHING HINT: When pop-ups are hit above the catcher, be sure he flips off his mask (if there is time) and turns his back to the pitcher before he catches the ball. Pop-ups have spin on them that carry them back toward the infield and are much easier to catch coming at the catcher rather than going away from him.

You now have about 25 minutes left in practice. Be sure to incorporate water breaks all of the time and especially on the hot days. Your players' health is your number one priority. For the final part of this practice have your pitchers throw to your hitters in a live situation. Put runners on base, start the batters with different counts and use different numbers of outs to work on different situations.

One situation I like to do is have a runner on second base with no outs and the batter needs to hit the ball to the right side of the infield to move the runner to third. Another situation is having the bases loaded with no outs and the count is one ball and two strikes. The batter needs to have a two-strike approach and focus on putting the ball in play to get the runner in from third. This situation also helps the defense. They have the choice of playing the corners in and settling for a double play up the middle, playing everyone in on the grass and trying to get the out at home or playing normal depth and making sure of getting one out while sacrificing a run. If a mistake happens during these situations then correct it immediately.

COACHING HINT: When you do live situations, be sure to have them written in your notebook so you can call them out immediately and not delay practice. As the season unfolds, keep notes on situations that happened in games so you can work on them in practice. This is the perfect time to understand what to do in these situations and when they happen again in a game...the results will fall in your favor!

Now that practice is over it is important for you to praise your team for their hard work, remind your team why you worked on the drills and how working on situations will help them in games. Also, let them know how they are better now than when practice first started and that you can't wait to be together again. Finish practice with a huddle and ask everyone to help with the gear and cleaning up the dugout. Thank them for being them.

Make a few minutes - while your mind is still fresh - to write notes about each player, how they did, what they need to keep working on for their IBP and write down ideas for the next practice. Be creative with your practice time and situations. Pay attention to the players' attitudes as some may be dragging and need inspiration. This is your team, your opportunity to get the best out of each player and help them succeed.

FOR THE BULLPEN IN YOUR BRAIN: Again, this is just one

sample of a practice that **simply** covered a lot of situations your team will encounter in games. Keep in mind, if a game were just batting practice and fielding drills...then that is all you would work on in practice. However, a baseball game is a human chess match and you need to know what to do with each move. So, practicing situations that will occur in games will **simply** put your team in the best position to succeed.

POSTGAME:
FINAL THOUGHTS

I can't thank you enough for being a baseball coach! When you apply the methods in this book then you will learn what works and what doesn't work for your players if you pay close attention to each player's IBP and pay attention to a player's mindset before good and bad experiences. When a player has a great practice or game you should know what transpired before suiting up and recreate it for him each day. If a player has a poor practice or game, remember he is human and next time work hard to redirect his mind to a positive state by helping him remember a great hit, pitch or a great play he made in his past!

Across our country, a little more than 6% of high school baseball players continue playing in college while receiving an education. If that number seems low to you, it is the second highest percentage of all high school sports except for hockey (11%). Only 5.7% of high school football players continue playing in college (and, there are more than 30,000 more college football than baseball players) and only 3% of high school basketball players play in college.

Put it this way...if you have 15 players on your baseball team, then *almost* one of them will continue playing in college. Less than 1/2 of 1% of high school players make it professionally in baseball. **So, coach to make each player the best he can be, create memories and let each player have fun while they can!** Let kids be kids because it won't be too long before they're in the real world...and, you know what that's like!

Now that you are ready to make a difference in a player's life, let's review all the *FOR THE BULLPEN IN YOUR BRAIN* sections and *COACHING HINTS* so you have them together in one spot:

FOR THE BULLPEN IN YOUR BRAIN: John Wooden is one of the greatest coaches of all time - in any sport - and he offered this to all the coaches in the world, *"Make sure that team members know they are working with you, not for you."*

FOR THE BULLPEN IN YOUR BRAIN: Are you determined to **always** plan so you can be your very best and so your players can be their very best? Hall of Famer Tommy Lasorda said, *"The difference between the impossible and the possible lies in a man's determination."*

FOR THE BULLPEN IN YOUR BRAIN: *"Things turn out best for the people who make the best of the way things turn out."* -- John Wooden

FOR THE BULLPEN IN YOUR BRAIN: Establish an IBP for each of your players, and for yourself, based on your definition of success and pay attention to what works. As Yogi Berra once said, *"You can observe a lot by just watching."*

FOR THE BULLPEN IN YOUR BRAIN: "It's the little details that are vital. Little things make big things happen." - John Wooden

FOR THE BULLPEN IN YOUR BRAIN: "I talked to the players and tried to make them aware of what was good and bad, but I didn't try to run their lives." - John Wooden

FOR THE BULLPEN IN YOUR BRAIN: During games become a "Strategic Coach" and a "Psychological Coach." A "Coaching Coach" is for practices.

FOR THE BULLPEN IN YOUR BRAIN: As a coach, it is really tough to please everyone on your team...and, their parents. However, simply **preparing for every situation** and living by your definition of success will allow you to sleep at night instead of tossing and turning and wondering, "What if?" Today's society is not as accountable as it used to be and the blame is tossed before looking in the mirror. Unfortunately, those who blame others tend to flock together. So, do your best to take that option away from them and rise above it all. You can make a difference and be a positive influence - on players AND parents - while the negative few soak in their tears until they get tired of it.

"Little League baseball is a very good thing because it keeps the parents off the streets." - Yogi Berra

FOR THE BULLPEN IN YOUR BRAIN: Great job, Coach! You just simplified the game of baseball to what it is really about...running, catching, throwing, fielding, hitting, sportsmanship and having fun. You stayed on time (which always makes the parents happy) and your team improved. The next step will define you as a coach. Once you see that everyone has a ride home, knows when the next practice or game is and the field looks as good as when you arrived...you need to make notes in your notebook for each player and his IBP. This will help you continue defining each player's IBP so you can help each one improve the next time you are together. Be sure to make a note of who got to hit first and even plan for who gets to hit first the next time. This should take you 5-15 minutes (while it is still fresh in your mind) and you have nearly written the plan for the next practice without taking more time out of your day.

If you can try to incorporate the same stations at every practice, modify them as needed, then your players will know what to expect.

Remember to take notes during games on situations your team needs to work on and recreate those situations in the next practice. This guarantees your players are meeting your definition of success.

Eventually, you can start having live batting practice with live situations. For example, remind them that getting the first out before a runner gets on base is your first goal. Then, it is **one out at a time**. The quicker you get three outs the quicker you get to hit! Until they play on a more competitive team, it really doesn't matter how they get the outs! When you can get this message across to your players you will have quick, effective practices that don't linger on and on and on.

"It gets late early out there." - Yogi Berra

FOR THE BULLPEN IN YOUR BRAIN: Great job, Coach! You just directed a productive practice, your players are better than they were when they arrived and you were able to discover what your team can do well and what skills need more attention. Before you head home or back to work, spend 5-15 minutes writing in your notebook about what you covered in practice, assessing your players' IBPs and what you want to cover the next time you step on the diamond. If you get in a habit of doing this while all your thoughts are fresh you will be rewarded with more time for yourself. Fight the temptation to just take ground balls and batting practice because you see that is what other teams are doing. You will have those practices, too. However, if you only take ground balls, fly balls and batting practice your players will be bored quickly, they will not perform well in games and you run the risk of losing your enthusiasm as a coach.

Remember, your team's job on defense is to get three outs as quickly as possible so they can get a chance to hit. Your team's job on offense is to put the ball in play to create more opportunities to score runs. It really is a **simple** game. You can simplify it more for your players by practicing actual situations they will have in games. Batting practice isn't what happens in a game so fight the temptation to spend too much time on it in practice. The only time batting practice happens in games is when your team isn't prepared to make three outs as quickly - and, **simply** - as possible.

"Victory or defeat is not determined at the moment of crisis, but rather in the long and unspectacular period of preparation."
- Anonymous

FOR THE BULLPEN IN YOUR BRAIN: Again, this is just one sample of a practice that **simply** covered a lot of situations your team will encounter in games. Keep in mind, if a game were just batting practice and fielding drills...then that is all you would work on in practice. However, a baseball game is a human chess match and you need to know what to do with each move. So, practicing situations that will occur in games will **simply** put your team in the best position to succeed.

COACHING HINT: If your first baseman is having troubles making plays...check his footwork first. Often times, first basemen get in a habit of stepping *before* the ball is being thrown to them and then they get stuck if the ball is not thrown exactly at their glove. If this is the case, remind them to step to the ball when it is in the air as

COACH LIKE A CHAMPION

if their glove had a string tied to the toe of their cleat.

COACHING HINT: One of my favorite things to do as a coach is steal the other team's signs. I thrive on it and I have our players try to figure them out, too! For those who are not in the first nine, this is a great way to keep them focused during a game. If you know your opponent's bunt coverage, then you can steal and fake bunt at the same time. They will be out of position and this gives you momentum to score more runs. If their third baseman is charging for a bunt and you have a runner on second base....call a steal and fake bunt! Nobody will be covering third base and you just advanced the runner without surrendering an out.

COACHING HINT: One important part of defending the squeeze bunt is making sure your third baseman sprints to home as soon as the runner on third takes off. You will have a better chance of getting the out at home plus your third baseman will be in a position to catch a bad bunt in the air and get a double play.

COACHING HINT: If you notice your outfielders are not very accurate with their throws...check their grips. Be sure they are using a four seam grip so the ball doesn't tail so much. They should be crow-hopping and throwing right at their target. Also, make sure they are catching the fly balls above their head and remind them that no line drive or ground ball gets by them...ever!

COACHING HINT: After an outfielder makes the perfect throw to home, praise him and ask him to lock that in his brain for when that same situation comes up in a game.

COACHING HINT: If you have an extra outfielder, have him stand in the batter's box with a helmet on and a bat so the catcher gets used to a batter being there. Have him stand in both sides of the box. Also, be sure your catcher is wearing all his gear so he gets used to throwing with it on.

COACHING HINT: When pop-ups are hit above the catcher, be sure he flips off his mask (if there is time) and turns his back to the pitcher before he catches the ball. Pop-ups have spin on them that carry them back toward the infield and are much easier to catch coming at the catcher rather than going away from him.

COACHING HINT: When you do live situations, be sure to have them written in your notebook so you can call them out immediately and not delay practice. As the season unfolds, keep notes on situations that happened in games so you can work on them in practice. This is the perfect time to understand what to do in these situations and when they happen again in a game...the results will fall in your favor!

COACHING AMERICA'S PASTIME...

RESPONSIBLE FOR AMERICA'S FUTURE

ABOUT THE AUTHOR
DREW COOLIDGE

Drew Coolidge is a High School State Champion baseball, golf and basketball coach in South Dakota. He also runs the Success Center for middle and high school students who need that extra support and confidence to become their very best.

When he is not coaching or teaching, Coolidge likes to spend time fly fishing in the beautiful Black Hills, researching sports success stories or getting his money worth on the golf course.

Coolidge is an active member of The Fellowship of Christian Athletes and is the FCA Huddle Leader at St. Thomas More High School.

You can contact Coolidge at www.CoachingBaseball101.com

This book is also available as an eBook on Amazon.com. Please spend one minute and leave a review of this book on Amazon.
Other eBooks by Drew Coolidge include:

'TWAS THE NIGHT BEFORE SPORTS...

SAY GOODBYE TO THE SLUMP

2013 WORLD SERIES: THE BIRDS AND THE BEARDS

www.ingramcontent.com/pod-product-compliance
Lightning Source LLC
Chambersburg PA
CBHW071639050426
42443CB00026B/767